THE ROLE OF GRACE

IN THE THOUGHT OF ALEXANDER CAMPBELL

WILLIAM J. RICHARDSON, PH.D.

**WESTWOOD CHRISTIAN FOUNDATION
FIRST ANNUAL RESTORATION LECTURES**

Wipf and Stock Publishers
Eugene, Oregon

Wipf and Stock Publishing
199 West 8th Avenue
Eugene, OR 97401

CONTENTS

ii

FOREWORD

One portion of the mission of the Westwood Christian Foundation in Los Angeles is devoted to lectures and symposia. A commitment to "Christian scholarly activity" was a part of the original intention of the Foundation. Also, from the beginning there has been a concern for the Reformation of the Nineteenth Century, which is the historical background of the Churches of Christ, Christian Churches and Christian Church (Disciples of Christ). The fragmentation of that movement and continued contact with leaders and friends in all segments of it has been a concern of the Foundation.

A part of the original dream of the Westwood Christian Foundation was an annual lectureship devoted to the thought and relevance of the Reformation of the Nineteenth Century. When the time came to develop such a lectureship, we began to think of those scholars most qualified to develop some relevant theme, both historically and with contemporary significance. The bicentennial of Alexander Campbell's birth was celebrated with a notable series of lectures by scholars from all major segments of the movement, sponsored by the Disciples of Christ Historical Society. It seemed timely to consider a theme that related the thought of Alexander Campbell to the contemporary scene. The doctrine of grace was selected, and immediately the name of Dr. William Richardson came to mind. He is a splendid scholar, and has been a dear friend for many years. His lecture in the bicentennial series, "Alexander Campbell As An Advocate of Christian Union," received the highest commendation from his peers. He was a natural choice. Dr. Richardson agreed to be the first lecturer for our new annual lectureship, scheduled for January 13-15, 1991.

Dr. Richardson holds the Bachelor of Theology degree from Northwest Christian College, the Bachelor of Divinity and Master of Arts degrees from Butler University, and the Doctor of Philosophy degree from the University of Oregon. He was Professor of New Testament and History at Northwest Christian College from 1947 to 1978, and Professor of Church History at Emmanuel School of Religion from 1978 to 1988 and he continues to serve Emmanuel as adjunct professor of Church history. Dr. Richardson is a seasoned scholar, who has done extensive work in research on the thought of Alexander Campbell. His high intellectual gifts are always expressed through a warm and congenial spirit.

We commend these lectures to you for your careful and thoughtful consideration. We believe Dr. Richardson has broken new ground and has called upon us all to give a major place to grace in our thinking. In the words of that celebrated scholar, James Moffatt, "All is of grace, and grace is for all." Never again should any of us preach on what we have called the plan of salvation—faith, repentance, confession, baptism—without giving due attention to grace. Without grace it is easy to slip into a legalism of self-salvation. What must I do to be saved is not a valid question, until first we ask what God has done to save us. These are vital and lively lectures for these days. When many of our preachers and leaders do not have an adequate historical perspective, and when many, especially among our younger preachers, are negative and sometimes antagonistic, lectures such as these are sorely needed. We send them forth with the fervent hope that they will help us to see the value of our historical heritage and enable us to discern its relevance to the times in which we live. We are all indebted to Dr. Richardson for his valuable and incisive contribution to the intellectual history of the Reformation of the Nineteenth Century.

Dr. Myron J. Taylor
Minister, Westwood Hills Christian Church
Ministerial Advisor, Westwood Christian Foundation

LECTURE I

GRACE AND THE FOEDUS NATURALE

(IN THE BEGINNING WAS GRACE)

The purpose of this presentation is to describe the relation of Alexander Campbell to covenant, or federal, theology, the predominant theology among churches of the Reformed tradition from the seventeenth to the nineteenth centuries. It was the theology of the Westminster Confession of Faith, and many of its overtones are present in much of Christian thought today. Campbell was nurtured in this theological tradition. Any analysis of his concept of grace must view the subject in the light of where he stood in relation to covenant theology.

Early in this century Hiram Van Kirk did an analysis of Campbell's theology[1] as part of a doctoral thesis at the University of Chicago. He rightly saw the crucial role the covenant idea played in Campbell's Biblical hermeneutics and quite clearly described Campbell's portrayal of Biblical covenants. However, he classified Campbell as a covenant theologian in the tradition of the chief representatives of that school, principally Johannes Cocceius. Not long after Van Kirk's work appeared, however, William Adams Brown brought forward the important distinction between the covenant idea itself and covenant theology. He recognized that the covenant idea permeates Biblical thought, chiefly but not exclusively in the Old Testament. Covenant theology, on the other hand, represents "a special type of Christian thought which gives this idea a central importance not elsewhere assigned to it, and uses it as the organizing principle of the entire theological system."[2] This distinction has proven to have merit; hence Van Kirk's

---

[1]Hiram Van Kirk, Rise of the Current Reformation (St. Louis, 1907); a few years earlier Winfred E. Garrison had devoted a chapter to Campbell's theological heritage which included an analysis of what he called covenant theology. Alexander Campbell's Theology (St. Louis, 1900).

[2]W. Adams Brown, "Covenant Theology," Encyclopedia of Religion and Ethics, IV, 216; Mark W. Karlberg, retains the term federalism but still distinguishes two types: 1) The speculative (the foedus naturale) and 2) that which is built along lines of the heilsgeschtliche approach to understanding Scripture. Mark W. Karlberg, "Reformed Interpretations of the Mosaic Covenant,"

identification of Campbell as a covenant theologian must be reappraised. Campbell rejected what has been shown to be the definitive element in federal theology—the concept of a covenant of works as the original covenant with man. There are, of course, other points as well in which he differed from Reformed views of the relation of the two testaments, but the above is most crucial in giving insight into the role of grace in his thought. The following analysis should provide the basis for understanding his views of this matter and the perspective from which he viewed the Gospel and role of obedience.

The general outlines of federal theology have been clearly drawn. It divided human history into two periods, each known by the type of covenant that defined man's relation to God. The first, the covenant of works, was made in the beginning with Adam and through him with the whole human race.[3] It promised life on the stipulation of perfect obedience to the Ten Commandments, thought to be identical with the law of nature and engraved upon the heart of man; hence, the designation, Foedus Naturale. For the most part federal theologians preferred to translate the Hebrew berith by the Latin foedus or pactum, which is bilateral, rather than by testamentum, which is unilateral in import.[4] The covenant was a "contractual arrangement, a divine-human quid pro quo."[5] Having been given to mankind at the beginning, the stipulations of the Decalogue are perpetually binding upon the whole of mankind, whether of the elect or not.[6] Edward Fisher, author of the Marrow of Modern Divinity (1645), endeavored to show that in eating the forbidden fruit Adam broke all the Ten Commandments.[7] But Adam's sin lay not

---

Westminster Theological Journal (Fall, 1980), 4

[3]Heinrich Heppe, Reformed Dogmatics, Set Out and Illustrated from the Sources, Revised by E. Bizer, Trans. by G. T. Thompson, (1950), 241

[4]John von Rohr, Covenant of Grace in Puritan Thought (1986), 37, declares that Puritan thinkers sought to hold these two concepts together in their concept of covenant.

[5]Ibid.

[6]Being "founded on the natural and immutable holiness of God," wrote Herman Witsius, these commands "cannot be abolished without abolishing the image of God." Economy of the Covenants between God and man, Trans. by W. Crookshank. 2 Vols. (1837) Book IV, Ch XIV, II. First published 1693.

[7]Edward Fisher, Marrow of Modern Divinity, (1650), 17-18.

alone in violating the Law; it was a denial of God's authority, hence a breach of fellowship. The consequences of the fall were guilt, corruption of human nature,[8] alienation from God, leaving man subject to indignation, wrath, and judgment.[9] Adam and his descendants were still obliged to keep the Law but in their lapsed state could not hope thereby to receive life.

Once the fall had occurred, even before their expulsion from the garden, God announced to Adam and Eve the covenant of grace (Genesis 3:15), which was to be in effect until the final judgment and which promises eternal life to the elect. This covenant was actually made with Christ as the Second Adam through whose perfect obedience these benefits are imputed to believers. The whole Biblical record from Genesis 3:15 onward is the story of the covenant of grace.

Both the Old Testament and the New Testament are economies of the covenant of grace—one in substance although different in administration.[10] These covenants are alike in the following particulars, according to Herman Witsius: 1) the contracting parties, God and man, are the same; 2) both promise eternal life; 3) both have the same conditions, faith and obedience to the law; 4) both have the glory of God as their final end.[11] The church is the same institution in both Testaments.

Although the elect are saved by God's mercy under the terms of the covenant of grace, the Law continues to play a foundational role. From creation onward all mankind are subject to its mandates. But there is a difference in the way its role was viewed, a difference of great importance to federal theologians. Fisher sought to clarify this matter in Marrow of Modern Divinity, in the dialogue between Evangelistica, Nomista, Antinomista, and Neophitis. He distinguished the Law of

---

[8]Prominent Puritan theologians refined this concept to mean that "depravity touched the whole range of human faculties, not that the total functioning of any or all the faculties was depraved." Von Rohr, 42. It is doubtful that such a refinement obtained among frontier revivalists of Campbell's time.

[9]Johannes Cocceius, De Foedus, III 63.

[10]Karl Barth assumes a similar position. While he refuses on critical grounds to fix the origin of the covenant in time, he still insists there is but one covenant of grace in scripture. In language reminiscent of the reformers he writes, "What is done away. . . is only its 'economy,' the form in which it [the covenant] is revealed and active in the events of the Old Testament." Church Dogmatics IV, 1, 32.

[11]Witsuis, Book I, Ch. I, XV.

Works, the Law of Faith, and the Law of Christ; but the Ten Commandments were the substance of each. The Law of Works was the covenant made with Adam, which promised life on the basis of perfect obedience; this covenant failed with Adam's disobedience. The Law of Faith is the covenant of grace by which Christ entered "into the same covenant of works that Adam did" and perfectly fulfilled it on our behalf.[12] This is the Gospel. The Law of Christ is the Ten Commandments, now serving as the rule of life for the elect.[13] Hence, he concluded, the Ten Commandments are the "matter of both covenants, only they differ in forms."[14]

The covenant of grace, although announced to Adam immediately after the fall, is actually grounded in an earlier pact between Father and Son, the covenant of redemption, in which even before creation the Son agreed to be redeemer of the elect and their mediator.[15] Thus the covenant of grace has both pretemporal and temporal aspects—pretemporal in that it was a pact entered into before creation, temporal in that it was implemented after the fall. Some theologians distinguished the covenant of redemption from the covenant of grace.[16] Witsius, however, preferred to see these two as periods of one covenant, the first being in the eternal counsel of the Trinity, the second in history "immediately upon the fall of man."[17]

What significance are we to see in this conception of the role of Christ in fulfilling perfectly the Law and incurring the penalty of disobedience to it—all on our behalf? Admittedly as John von Rohr states, it "gave a Christological foundation to the covenant of grace."[18] But it is difficult to resist the conclusion drawn by David Alexander Wier that the covenant of grace is "really therefore the

---

[12]Marrow, 27.

[13]"The Law of Christ in regard to substance and matter is . . . summed up in the Decalogue . . . commonly called The Moral Law." Ibid. 61

[14]Ibid., 68

[15]von Rohr, 43; Heppe, 374-377; Fisher, 27; Witsius, Book II, Ch. II, I

[16]von Rohr, 45

[17]Witsius, Book II, Ch. III, I-III

[18]von Rohr, 44

covenant of works in disguise."[19]

Covenant theology in the above particulars represents a development distinct not only from the early reformers, particularly John Calvin, but also from the Reformed Scholasticism that arose a generation after him.

On the one hand, it was an attempt to reconcile the Reformed doctrine of God's sovereignty and the fall of Adam, that is, the view that God's providence "extended over the fall."[20] The harshness commonly associated with Calvinism is the product of the age that followed him—an age that saw the rise of Reformed scholasticism which, beginning with the premise of God's absolute sovereignty and viewing Scripture as a body of propositions, proceeded by logical deduction to construct a system whose effect was to give to Calvinism a face that would have seemed strange to the Geneva reformer himself.[21] Under the impact of this system, to quote Charles Sherwood McCoy, "The divine-human relationship was in danger of becoming the theological counterpart of the emerging understanding of the world as a machine."[22] Calvin had made predestination a matter for consideration under Soteriology; however, the later "Calvinists" placed it under Theology Proper, thus making predestination the keystone of their system.[23]

In an effort to "mitigate the rigor of Reformed Scholastic Theology" covenant theology introduced the element of contingency into the relation of God

---

[19]David Alexander Wier, Foedus Naturale: The Origins of Federal Theology in Sixteenth Century Reformation Thought. Unpublished doctoral dissertation, University of St. Andrews (1984), 7

[20]Ibid., 76

[21]Charles Sherwood McCoy, The Covenant Theology of Johannes Cocceius, a Ph.D. dissertation, (Yale), 1957, University Microfilm, Ann Arbor) 8; Everett Emerson, "Calvin and Covenant Theology," Church History (June, 1956), 138-139; Wier, 85-87; von Rohr, 3, asserts that "Calvin himself was not a good Calvinist."

[22]McCoy, 83

[23]von Rohr, 3-430; Weir, 56. The effect of this development is described by McCoy as follows: "This strong emphasis on the single act of divine will before creation tends to render meaningless the interaction between God and man described in Scripture and to weaken, if not destroy, the significance of history and of salvation through historical events." Charles Sherwood McCoy, "Johannes Cocceius, Federal Theologian," Scottish Journal of Theology (Dec. 1963), 366

to man.[24] It sought, according to von Rohr, to retain two Protestant principles: "the voluntarism inherent in Protestantism's call for faith and obedience as the believer's response to God's proclaimed word" and the Protestant "emphasis upon God's sovereignty... unconditionally determining human destiny."[25]

A second factor, often cited, in the rise of covenant theology was the concern of sixteenth and seventeenth century political philosophers to find a theological basis for the duty of man in the natural realm. The covenant of grace as conceived by the early reformers involved only the elect, hence laid no basis for a social-political theory for society as a whole. By invoking the idea of a prior covenant, one in substance with the law of nature, a basis for structuring society could be found which was incumbent upon all men, saved or not.[26]

Federal theology represents a movement not only away from Reformed scholasticism but also a marked shift away from Calvin.[27] Calvin knew but one covenant, the covenant of grace, which he believed was of the same substance in both the Old and New Testaments.[28] He did not speak of a pre-lapsarian covenant of works.[29] There is evidence that he regarded the situation of Adam and Eve in the

---

[24]Emerson, 139

[25]von Rohr, 1, 30

[26]Leonard Trinderud credits the Rhineland theologians, Ursinus and Olevianus, with utilizing this mode of thought in forming the concept of a foedus naturale between God and Adam and his descendants but states that the roots for the idea of "authority grounded in natural law and social contract" are late medieval. Leonard J. Trinderud, "The Origins of Puritanism," Church History (March, 1951), 38-42; cp. James B. Torrence, "Covenant or Contract," Scottish Journal of Theology (Feb. 1970), 61; Van Kirk, 36-40, cites the influence of Hugo Grotius.

[27]Some, however, argue that covenant theology, as set forth in the Westminster Confession of Faith, is a consistent development of Calvin's thought. See Paul Helm, "Calvin and the Covenant, Unity, and Continuity." Evangelical Quarterly (April, 1983), 66; cf Emerson "Calvin and Covenant Theology," 141

[28]Institutes, II, 11, 2-4

[29]Jens G. Moeller, "The Beginnings of Puritan Covenant Theology," Journal of Ecclesiastical History, (April, 1963), 49-50; Torrence, 61-62

Garden as a state of grace.[30]

Scholarly opinion differs over who merits the distinction of being first to put forth the scheme that called for a pre-lapsarian covenant of works. Some credit Heinrich Bullinger (1504-1575) with being the first advocate of federalism.[31] There is, however, general agreement that Heidelberg theologians, Zachary Ursinus and Casper Olevianus, were the "most prominent of the sixteen century federalists."[32] Recognized as the most able expositor of Scripture predicated on the federalist principle is Johannes Coccceius (1603-1669)[33] It also found able exponents in William Ames (1576-1633) and Herman Witsius, whose Economy of the Covenants between God and Man (1685) represents covenant theology in its "later and more developed form."[34] Covenant Theology was second nature to Puritans on both sides of the Atlantic. Important to our understanding of Campbell is the fact that the Church of Scotland and its affiliates "upheld the system in its utmost consistency and extremest form."[35]

The developed covenant theology was formalized as an article of faith in the Westminster Confession of Faith, which clearly distinguishes the covenants of works and grace. Some contend that this article is a legitimate development of Calvin's thought.[36] Leonard J. Trinderud, however, states that this confession and the Shorter and Larger Catechisms are the "only official Reformed and Calvinistic symbols which embody the federal scheme." He states further that these documents

---

[30]Wier, 12-13

[31]McCoy, Covenant Theology of Coccceius, 64-65; Mark W. Karlberg, 8-12; Wier, 13-14, disputes this interpretation.

[32]Karlberg, 17; cf Trinderud, 48; Wier, 3-4

[33]Karl Barth: "Coccceius represents the Federal Theology in a form which is not only most perfect, but also the ripest and strongest and most impressive." Dogmatics IV, 1, 60

[34]Brown, 227

[35]C. P. Wing, "Federal Theology" McClintock and Strong, Cyclopedia, III, 519

[36]Helm, 1

show "the essential genius of the federal scheme against that of Calvin."[37]

While federal theologians differed from early reformers in contending for an Edenic covenant of works, they agreed with them in the threefold function of the Law: the civil, pedagogical, and the regulative.[38] Fisher reflected these usages in the Marrow of Modern Divinity.

> The law of Christ in regard to substance and matter is all one
> with the law of works, or covenant of works. .. summed up in the
> Decalogue. .. commonly called The Moral Law .... Therefore was
> it given of God to be a true and eternal rule of righteousness, for
> all men of all nations, and at all times....[39]

In the work of Coccerius federal theology made a distinct contribution to the development of the Reformed tradition. He gave a systematic presentation of the federalist scheme, holding together predestination and human responsibility.[40] His concern for careful exegesis prepared the way for modern critical Biblical studies. While not completely free from the excesses of Reformed scholasticism he sought, in Barth's words, "to understand the work and word of God attested in Holy Scripture dynamically and not statically, as an event and not as a system of objective and self-contained truths."[41] Gottleb Shrenk credits Coccerius with preparing "the way for. . . Biblical Theology."[42] McCoy ranks him among those great minds who provided "the church with a full-scale philosophy of history" with roots in the progressive unfolding of the covenant of God through its successive

---

[37]Trinderud, 52; Wier supports this assessment and illustrates it by comparing the Helvetic Confession and the Larger Catechism, produced by the Westminster divines. Wier, 181-182.

[38]As civil law it restrains the wicked and provides the order necessary both for social life and for proclamation of the gospel; as 'theological' law, it bares before us the enormity of our sin." Justo L. Gonzolaz, History of Christian Thought (Nashville, 1975) III, 46-47. The regulative function was guidance of the life of the believer.

[39]Fisher, 154

[40]Torrence, 68

[41]Barth, IV, 55

[42]Quoted in McCoy, Covenant Theology of Coccerius, 94

stages culminating in Christ.[43]

The federal system, however, has been severely criticized at several crucial points, certain of which are appropriate to our understanding of Campbell's rejection of the premise on which it was grounded.

The notion of a pre-temporal pact of redemption between Father and Son, while it appears to emphasize the role of grace, does not take from the Law its pivotal role in the purpose of God. According to federal theology man from the beginning was subject to the Law (the covenant of works) and was therefore a "legal creature." Mankind's obligation to the Law still remains even though people cannot achieve life through it. The sin which was remedied by Christ's life of perfect obedience and sacrificial death was man's breach of the Law. Hence in a real sense, as Wier writes, "The covenant of works is ... the primary covenant which God has made with man."[44]

Karl Barth presents what to me is the most thorough critique of covenant theology, based upon his analysis of Cocceius. Not all his observations bear upon our present concern, which is to state where Campbell stood in relation to covenant theology. I cite what I consider his most telling objections to the scheme.

The fundamental problem for Barth is the tension arising from the concept of two covenants both bearing upon man's relation to God, yet built upon two separate principles, one, the covenant of Law or Works—derived from nature, the other, deriving from grace. "The rivalry of the two principles," writes Barth, "cannot be overcome."[45] Putting the covenant of works first in time, he writes, resulted in the covenant of grace being viewed as a "covenant of grace only in antithesis" to the covenant of works; the covenant of works, as the original covenant, became "the framework and standard of reference for the covenant of grace." What sin is "is measured by the Law of the first covenant," and the "decisive gift" brought to man in the covenant of grace is that Christ as the second Adam fulfills that Law in our place. The upshot of this is that the Law continues to retain its relevance, and the quid pro quo relationship between man and God so basic to the covenant of works threatens to retain its force under the covenant of

---

[43]Ibid., 94-95

[44]Weir, 8

[45]Barth, IV, 59

grace.[46]

James B. Torrence voices the same complaint, asserting that federal theology did not escape the legalism implicit to the emphasis upon Law in the first covenant. Although the covenant of grace was presumed to be unconditioned it became confused with contract, leading to the notion of "conditional grace."[47] Torrence cites the Marrow of Modern Divinity in support of this point; for while that document reflected the federalist view of the role of the Law, its aim was to recover Reformed thought from the tendency to see grace as conditional. The rejection of the "Marrow" party by the eighteenth century Church of Scotland is evidence that the "contractual" notion was still very much in vogue in that part of Great Britain.[48]

Barth also raises serious questions about the idea of a pre-temporal intertrinitarian pact (the so-called covenant of redemption) between Father and Son. One question has to do with the propriety of the Edenic covenant of works in the light of this prior covenant within "the bosom of the Godhead itself." He asks:

> When the supreme basis was ascribed to the covenant of grace, how was it thought possible that another covenant, the foedus naturale or operum [the covenant of works], could be placed alongside it and even given precedence over it?[49]

and again:

---

[46]Barth elaborates further: "In spite of assurances to the contrary, this side of the eschaton ... there is no effective abrogation of the covenant of nature and works either in the Old Testament and consequently in the New. For the New Testament freedom is only freedom from the Law of the Old Testament. . . but the validity of the Law of that first covenant is the guiding thread that runs through the whole development. Grace itself, whether as justification or sanctification, is always the fulfilling of the Law. . . . There is no escape from the relationship of du ut des [I give so that you may give]." Barth, IV, 62-63

[47]Torrence, 66. H. Richard Niebuhr sees a common trend in this direction: "The tendency of the covenant idea to degenerate into the limited contract idea is evident in all the later religious and social history." "The Idea of Covenant in American Democracy." Church History, (June, 1954), 135; von Rohr, on the other hand, believes that Puritans generally managed to avoid this tendency.

[48]See Stewart Mechie, "The Marrow Controversy Re-visited," Evangelical Quarterly (Jan. 1950)

[49]Barth, IV, 63

> Why is there ascribed to him [Adam] a status in which he did not
> need the mediator and which, if it had lasted, would have made
> superfluous the appearance of the mediator and therefore the
> fulfilment of the eternal (!) covenant of grace?[50]

The effect of the covenant of works, he concludes, was to make the grace of God
"a second or third thing, a wretched expedient of God in face of the obvious failure
of a plan in relation to man which had originally had quite a different intention and
form."[51]

Barth is further troubled by the implications of the pre-temporal pact
between Father and Son for our understanding of the being of God. On the one hand
it suggests that an "inter-trinitarian arrangement and contract" was necessary to
"establish the unity of the righteousness and mercy of God in relation to man.... It
is only with the conclusion of this contract with Himself that He ceases to be a
righteous God in abstracto and becomes the God who in His righteousness is also
merciful and therefore able to exercise grace." In addition, this concept of an
intertrinitarian pact has serious implications for our understanding of the Trinity
itself. It conveys the idea of the "first and second persons of the triune godhead as
two divine subjects and therefore as two legal subjects who can... enter into
obligations one with another." Such a view, he declares, has "no place in a right
understanding of the Trinity."[52]

Most critical for Barth is the fact that the intertrinitarian pact which is the
basis for the covenant of grace and which is initiated presumably for the sake of
men's salvation, is "made in absence of the one who must be present as the second
partner at the institution of the covenant to make it a real covenant, that is, man."[53]

We turn our attention now to the way Campbell, as a rebellious son of the
Scottish reformation, understood the implications of federal theology for the
Biblical doctrine of grace. Campbell was certainly a covenant thinker. Though his
ideas differed somewhat from the federalist scheme, they still reflect its impact upon
him in such matters as his emphasis upon the history of salvation and upon the role
of covenants in the development of God's purposes. He employed much of the
terminology and many of the concepts of federal theology. It is understandable that
Van Kirk identified him as a covenant theologian.

---

[50]Ibid., 64

[51]Ibid.

[52]Ibid., 64-65

[53]Ibid., 66

However, the few points at which Campbell differed from covenant theology are of such significance as to justify the conclusion he was not a covenant theologian, and he was explicit in saying so. The views of the Law being then held in England and in Scotland, he wrote, "belong much more to speculations and scholastic theology than to the elements of the Gospel, or the worship of the Christian Church."[54]

First, he rejected the keystone of federal theology—the concept of a pre-lapsarian covenant of works comprising the Decalogue and obligatory upon all mankind. Many "insipid volumes" he declared, had been written on the Ten Commandments.

> Some have called it the Moral Law and made it the law of the whole spiritual kingdom, affirming that Adam was created under it, and that even the angels were under it as a rule of life; nay, that it is now, and ever will be, the law of the whole spiritual world.... Though it speaks of fathers, mothers, wives, and children, houses and lands, slaves, and cattle, murder, theft, and adultery; yet it is the moral code of the universe."[55]

In light of his rejection of a pre-lapsarian covenant of works Campbell saw no place in the Christian system for the concept of a pre-temporal pact of redemption between the Father and Son, as precursor of the covenant of grace. There was a pretemporal plan of God to establish the Kingdom of Heaven under the headship of his Son. But Campbell's view of the godhead did not allow him to be comfortable speaking of Father and Son in the pre-temporal context-except by way of anticipation of the Incarnation. Hence, any "understanding and agreement" as there was "ere time began" was "between God and the Word of God—or, as now revealed between the Father and the Son."[56]

Moreover, he did not accept the oft-repeated maxim of covenant theology

---

[54]Millennial Harbinger, (1835), 551; hereafter MH

[55]Christian Baptist, Burnet edition, One Volume, (Aug. 1829), 574. Hereafter CB. Campbell did find in the two commandments, Love of God, Love of neighbor, principles of universal obligation, which are "engraven with more or less clearness on every human heart" and "constitute the conscience of man." MH (1846), 500. All men posses this "sense of right and wrong" although in "varying degrees according to... circumstances." Ibid., 519. But he explicitly denied that the Ten Commandments, although based upon these principles, were either identical with them or operative in man's original state.

[56]MH (1834), 406

that while Christians are not under the Law as a covenant of works they are subject to it as their rule of life. He asserted this position as early as 1816 in the Sermon on the Law; then as later it evoked indignant response from elements in the Reformed Tradition.[57]

Finally, federal theologians had incorporated into their system the view of the early reformers that there is but one covenant of grace under two testaments. Campbell would grant that grace is the constant element in all God's actions in reference to man; but God had established different covenants in carrying out his purpose. Failure so to recognize these covenants had produced much confusion. Referring specifically to the Mosaic and Christian institutions he wrote: "The Holy Spirit calls them 'two covenants' or "two institutions' and not two modifications of one covenant."[58] It might appear that his insistence upon distinguishing Old Testament and New Testament as covenants rather than accepting the conventional Reformed phrasing is a distinction without significance. But to Campbell failure to make such a distinction had resulted in giving undue importance to the Law in Christianity and also in making other Old Testament institutions normative to the church today. On one occasion he listed nearly a dozen such instances.[59]

The above complaints against federal theology appear in Campbell's correspondence with editor William Jones of London, England. The latter had expressed dismay at Campbell's views of the Law set forth in an early issue of the Christian Baptist.[60] Jones voiced the usual rationale for the federalist position and called upon the editor of the Millennial Harbinger to acknowledge his error. Specifically he affirmed that the Law is the "eternal rule of righteousness.... founded on the very nature of God...a transcript of holiness, justice, and goodness." The law was "written on the heart of Adam as the law of creation." Moreover, he declared, it is only as "forming a part of the old covenant" that it is done away; it still serves as the rule of life for believers. In his response Campbell rebutted each of these

---

[57]MH (1846), 509; see his response to Mr. Brantly of the Columbian Star, Ibid., (1830), 81-65, and his epistolary exchange with R. B. Semple, Ibid., (1831), 8-16

[58]Christian System, 116. In Christian Baptism (1853), 331, he characterized the notion of "two dispensations of one covenant" as "dust and ashes thrown by theological doctors into the eyes of the too credulous devotees."

[59]CB (Aug. 1823), 9

[60]Quoted in MH (1835), 540-541

arguments.[61] Elsewhere in these epistolary exchanges he stated his misgivings about Jones' notion of a covenant made with the elect "dated from all eternity." That God had in mind such a covenant was for Campbell the teaching of Scripture but not the notion of such a covenant actually made with the elect "<u>before</u> Christ died, sometime dated from all eternity." The latter would not be a new covenant at all but the "oldest and first of all covenants."[62]

The covenant idea figured prominently into Campbell's writings and addresses throughout his career. He set forth what is probably his most mature understanding of covenant in one of an extended series of "Tracts for the People," (1846).[63] God's plan for the universe is the context for understanding the covenants in the Scriptures. The Bible shows a "plan of a gradual and progressive development adopting itself to all the conditions of human existence." God's purpose is "the communication of himself to his intelligent and moral offspring." The "vehicle" by which he manifests his creative powers is his word. Man's nature is such that he needs "some supreme constitution, or law, or covenant, by which his Sovereign and himself can understand each other and maintain perpetual amity;" he must, said Campbell, have a covenant. It is through a succession of covenants, which Campbell here called "covenants of promise" that God fulfills his providential and redemptive purpose. Hence the hermeneutical key to the message of the "inspired volume" is the understanding of the various covenants through which that purpose is carried out. In this treatise Campbell identified nine covenants in the Hebrew Scriptures; earlier in his debate with Walker, he had identified only seven.[64] It is beyond our purpose to analyze these covenants; but it is important to

---

[61]<u>Ibid.</u>, 551-557

[62]<u>Ibid.</u>, 459

[63]<u>Ibid.</u>, (1846), 252-255. He later incorporated this treatise in <u>Christian Baptism</u> (1853).

[64]<u>Debate on Christian Baptism between Mr. John Walker. . .and Alexander Campbell</u> (1822), 6-11; hereafter <u>Campbell-Walker Debate</u>. Campbell regarded three of these covenants, the covenant with Noah, the promise to Abraham concerning Christ, and the covenant with David, as being without conditions hence incapable of being broken.

Barth emphasizes the historical character of revelation but refuses to locate that revelation in specific events. Therefore he objects to Cocceius' "historicizing" the revelation and would undoubtedly express the same objection to Campbell's approach as well. In my opinion, critical questions aside, we should consider what

note that he identified all of them as covenants of grace or mercy.

Although he continued to use the term <u>covenant</u> Campbell believed that <u>berith</u> and <u>diathēkē</u> should be rendered by terms that reflect God's initiative. Covenants involving the divine-human relationship are not <u>synthēkē</u>–agreements "upon the principle of stipulation and restipulation." Rather, <u>diathēkē</u>, as the rendering of <u>berith</u> in the Septuagint and as the term employed in the New Testament signifies an "institution, or declaration of <u>will, purpose, promise</u>," hence is most appropriate to a relationship where God stipulates everything requiring only that man accede to the terms in order to participate in the blessing promised.[65] This divine initiative underscores the affirmation that grace underlay the acts of God from the beginning.[66]

A number of words served to translate the original Biblical terms: precept,

---

the tradition is trying to say.

[65]Recent scholarly studies have tended to establish the antiquity of the practice of covenant making. Researchers have found in ancient suzerainity treaties models for understanding Old Testament covenants. These treaties embodied features such as the following: the statement of the terms is monopleural, that is, set forth by the superior party. It is not a negotiated arrangement. Still, however, the inferior party must agree to the terms to put the covenant into effect. The treaty itself contains several elements: reference to the history of the relationship of the two parties, stipulations, and promises of blessings for adherence to the treaty (or curses for non-observance). See Delbert R. Hillers, <u>Covenant, the History of a Biblical Idea</u>, (Baltimore, 1969)

Campbell was unaware of, or at least did not make reference to, the suzerainity model. But his concept of covenant closely resembles the latter in the following particulars: the initiative lies with God, who lays down the stipulations and promise of blessing. The covenantees become so related by their acceptance of these terms. The covenant is predicated upon the history of the relationship of the parties, namely, the redemptive acts of God.

Campbell also recognized, as do recent scholars, that there are some covenants, in the Old Testament particularly, in which there are <u>no</u> stipulations—only promises—on God's part, namely the covenants with Noah, Abraham, David.

[66]"We, therefore, affirm that the remedial system in its inception, progress, and consummation is all of grace." <u>MH</u> (1857, 390-391; (1846), 255-256. Campbell expressed these views as early as 1820 in his debate with Walker. Campbell-<u>Walker Debate</u>, 153-154, 165-166

promise, appointment, dispensation, charter, constitution, institution. He wavered in preference between <u>constitution</u> and <u>institution</u> but in later years opted for the latter.[67] In referring to these successive divine arrangements in the history of salvation he used such titles as "covenants of mercy," "covenants of grace," or "institutions of favor."

Campbell's deviation from federal theology did not rest primarily upon the contrast he drew between the Law and the Gospel in the Sermon on the Law. The attitudes toward the Law to which he objected in that document are indeed those cherished by covenant theologians and central to the Reformed tradition. But only at a few points in that sermon did he allude to specific tenets of covenant theology, notably the concept of a covenant of works and the corresponding notion of Gentiles being subject to the Ten Commandments as the embodiment of the law of nature.

The crucial point at which to compare Campbell and covenant theology is in his attitude toward Adams's status in Eden, where he represented (as federal head) the whole human race. Was Adam—and after him all mankind—subject to the Ten Commandments? Is his relation to God properly described as a <u>quid pro quo</u>, in which he was offered life on the basis of perfect obedience to that Law? Is Adam's sin to be understood primarily by reference to his relation to God or by his relation to the Law? Does grace enter the picture historically only after the fall?

Only reluctantly did Campbell refer to the arrangement in Paradise as a covenant, but he was willing to accommodate to common usage on the grounds that the arrangement in the Garden was a charter or institution of divine appointment.[68] Eden was a state of grace, an inheritance "freely bestowed upon Adam, irrespective of any thought, volition, or deed on his part. . ... his possession of it was of pure favor."[69] Campbell was categorical in denying that this was a covenant of works.

> This has sometimes been theologically called a covenant of works, in contrast with a covenant of grace. But there were no works prescribed in this institution. It was a charter, a stipulation, and a guarantee of <u>liberty</u> and <u>life</u> to man.[70]

There was, however, one command set forth as a condition for Adam's enjoyment of this status.

---

[67]<u>MH</u> (1857), 391

[68]<u>Campbell-Walker Debate</u>, 154; <u>MH</u> (1846), 256

[69]<u>MH</u> (1832), 251

[70]<u>Ibid.</u>, (1846), 256

He held this estate by a grant from his creator, not a condition of his paying one barley corn per annum, but on condition of his obedience to one positive command which, to make it still more divinely generous, required not the doing of any thing, but the simple withholding of his hand from the fruit of a single tree.[71]

Campbell followed some earlier Reformed thinkers in regarding this sanction simply as a test of Adam's loyalty.[72]

Campbell's attitude toward federal theology was a principal mark of his separation from the Westminster tradition in which he had been reared. But he was moved not simply by the lack of Biblical warrant for a pre-lapsarian covenant of works but by the conviction that the grace made incarnate in Jesus of Nazareth had from the beginning set in motion and guided God's progressive dealings with mankind.

References to the grace of God abound in Campbell's works. He held the commonly accepted meaning of the term, expressed in such equivalents as favor and mercy. He did, however, differ from his Reformed forebears by his refusal to associate the meaning of grace with the effectual calling by the Spirit of those who have been divinely elected.[73] Notwithstanding his rejection of the doctrine of particular election Campbell agreed that grace describes the divine initiative in our salvation. This is illustrated in his well-known treatise on the Kingdom of Heaven. In the concluding portion of this essay he distinguished two categories of the "blessings of God bestowed on man," which he called "the antecedent and consequent."

In the kingdom of heaven the antecedent blessings are the constitution [covenant] of grace, the King, and all he did, suffered, and sustained for our redemption. These were finished before we came upon the stage of action. This is the favor, pure favor, sovereign favor; for there can be no favor that is not free and sovereign.[74]

The above statement, adapted to the terms of the charter given to Adam, fitly describes the first covenant ever made with mankind. It was a charter of grace, as

---

[71]MH (1832), 251; cf. Ibid., (1830), 107

[72]Ibid., (1830), 107; (1840), 75. Campbell resembled Calvin more than the federal theologians in his understanding of the original status of man.

[73]Westminster Confession of Faith, Ch III, V; Ch X, I, II; Ch XI, III

[74]MH (1834), 424-425

were all the covenants that succeeded it in time.

David Alexander Wier has observed that while federal theology originated with "questions about God, his nature, and his relation to man and the universe," it had implications "sometimes more important and more far reaching than its origins." He refers to such matters as the "theology of the sacraments, the relationship between church and state, the morphology of conversion. .., the doctrine of justification, and Christian ethics."[75] The same may be said of Campbell's rejection of federal theology and his corresponding emphasis upon covenants of grace in Scripture beginning with the charter given to Adam. Covenant as a principle of interpretation and grace as indicative of the intention of God in history became the key to Campbell's understanding of the religion of the Bible. For Campbell: in the beginning was grace.

---

[75] Wier, 167

LECTURE II

GRACE AND THE GOSPEL

If Alexander Campbell were asked to encapsulate in a word the nature and purpose of God as revealed in the Hebrew and Christian Scriptures, he would undoubtedly have used the word grace. Grace was a constant emphasis in his speaking and writing from the earliest days to the twilight of his career. The following statement, made in 1851, is typical: "Salvation, in the aggregate, is all of grace, and all its parts are consequently gracious."[1] For Campbell grace underlay not only the creation but the whole scheme of redemption from its inception, whether contemplated in terms of the acts of God in fulfillment of his purpose or the appointed acts persons are called upon to make in response. Before the foundation of the world, he wrote, "the whole remedial. . . system was purposed, arranged, and established upon the basis of the revealed distinctions of Father, Son, and Holy Spirit." It went through stages of development "in the different ages of the world," involving a variety of institutions—all to fulfill God's gracious purpose.[2] Thus, Eden was a state of grace. The successive covenants and the institutions associated with each were likewise covenants of grace or mercy. This was true even of the Mosaic covenant. Even though in tracing the history of salvation he classified it as the dispensation of law as distinct from the "reign of favor" in Christ,[3] the Mosaic covenant nonetheless was in its turn a covenant of mercy.

In supreme manifestation the grace of God was incarnate in Jesus Christ. "The Gospel" he wrote, "is emphatically the grace of God . . . the favor of God towards sinners—this is no where so fully exhibited as in the gift of his Son."[4]

The Gospel as "the favor of God towards sinners" suggests that the goal of God's grace in history is the recovery of man from the state and consequences of sin. It also reflects the seriousness of sin. In 1830, Campbell began a series entitled "History of Sin." In his introduction he identified two extremes regarding

---

[1]MH (1851), 325

[2]Christian System, 18-19

[3]Ibid., 154

[4]CB (1825), 137

sin, one which "expatiates upon its demerit until language fails," the other "always extenuating its malignity." He made this observation:

> To those who labor to diminish our abhorrence of sin, Christianity and all its wondrous works of mercy and favor appear an unnecessary and extravagant display about nothing; but to those who contemplate it in the light which revelation pours upon it, everything in the economy of mercy attests the wisdom and favor of God displayed in the Gospel.[5]

But what to him was the most malign of all sins is that of rebellion, either of angel or man, saying to the Lord of the universe, "Thou shalt not reign over me." In Campbell's thinking, what made Adam's sin different from every sin "since committed" was that it was "the sin of a perfect man" while "all other sins are the sins of sinful men."[6]

Mr. Campbell's understanding of the consequences of the fall did not differ substantially from those in the Reformed tradition; the fall affected man's nature and brought estrangement from God. But he differed sharply from the Reformed position, especially as it had developed in the centuries following the great reformers, over the question of the nature and extent of man's disability and the way divine grace operates in remedying man's situation, and indeed, over the nature of grace itself.

In one of a series of "Essays on Man in his Primitive State," begun in 1828, Campbell asserted that man by his fall lost the image of God. By this he meant "loss of a correct idea of God's image" and of "his conformity to it"—a loss of his personal glory.[7] Again in "History of Sin" he spoke of man's nature as "impaired and debased."[8] The Christian System contains a similar estimate; the natural (man's original estate) had become "preternatural."[9]

A more comprehensive statement, emphasizing loss of fellowship with God along with disability in man's nature appears in one of a series, "Tracts for the

---

[5]MH (1830) 106-107. Of the eight articles in this series Campbell wrote only three, quoting J. Whelply, Lectures upon Ancient History for the remainder of the series.

[6]Ibid., 107-109

[7]CB (1828), 484-485

[8]MH (1830), 109.

[9]Christian System, 14-16

People" begun in 1845 and extending over a four year period. In it he wrote that as a result of his apostasy man "lost three things—union with God, original righteousness, and original holiness." The goal of the remedial system, which originates in the unmerited favor of God, "is a nearer, more intimate, and more sublime union with God. . .[as] enduring as eternity."[10]

Campbell acknowledged the problem of how to account for the fact that one man's rebellion should transmit its effects to all his children. However difficult to explain, he observed, the fact remains that a "disease in the moral constitution of man is as clearly transmissible as any physical trait, if there be any truth in history, biography, or human observation."[11]

What was more important to him was the conviction that man could be restored. Restoration is the goal of all God has done in addressing himself to mankind since the fall. Concerning the state of man after the fall he asserted that Adam did not lose "susceptibility of being restored to the image of God.[12] This conviction lay behind his rejection of the concept of total depravity as it had come to be held in Reformed thought and especially in the revivalism of the Second Great Awakening. The Westminster Confession of Faith identified grace as irresistible, the direct operation of the Holy Spirit upon the heart, effectively calling the elect to faith; until this occurs the sinner is "in natural bondage to sin." The Holy Spirit "quickens and renews" the elect so that they are able to answer the call.[13] Grace thus become "sovereign" or "free and special."

Campbell recognized grace as sovereign but objected to its exercise being particularized as in the Reformed doctrine of election. Although he often used the phrase free and sovereign grace he thought it was in effect redundant to add the prefixes free and sovereign, since he believed these qualities naturally belong to the term. But he refused to attach to these prefixes the meaning given to them in the Westminster standard. Such a view, which identified grace with the Spirit's irresistible operation, made grace "a sort of fluid, resembling the electric, which bursts from the clouds that pass over our fields."[14]

Campbell could assert human depravity. But man was not totally depraved,

---

[10]MH (1849), 363

[11]Christian System, 15

[12]CB (1828), 484).

[13]Westminster Confession of Faith, Ch. IX, II, Ch. X, IV

[14]CB (1825), 137

for this would mean that each person is as corrupted as Satan himself; nor could the concept of total depravity square with the Biblical idea of persons becoming worse and worse. To assert total depravity and irresistibility of grace was to make grace "incompatible with human instrumentality."[15]

The effect of this theology, in what was popularly known as "experimental religion" in early nineteenth century revivals, was to make regeneration an ontological change necessarily antecedent to and therefore separate from faith. A change in one's nature must occur before one could believe. In the Christian Baptist for 1824 Campbell cited the testimonial of a preacher that he had been regenerated three years before he believed in Christ; he described himself as having been "born again by a physical energy of the Holy Spirit." He was for those three years a "godly unbeliever," but had he died he would have been saved.[16] Although an extreme example it illustrates the type of experience contemplated in the revivialist view of man and the grace of God.

Campbell regarded the term salvation as also describing the goal of divine grace in the scheme of redemption. In substance, as he understood these terms, restoration of man and salvation are the same. He did, however, recognize latitude in the use of the term salvation in scripture: it could apply to temporal matters, as in the deliverance of Israel from Egypt, to one's spiritual life, or to one's eternal state. As it concerned the effects of sin in personal life, salvation meant "pardon of sin or deliverance from the pollution and dominion of sin. . . and eternal salvation of the whole man from every trace and every consequence of sin."[17]

> . . . when a person becomes Christ's, he is a son of Abraham, an heir, a brother, or is pardoned, justified, sanctified, reconciled, and saved.
>
> To be in Christ, or under Christ, then, is to stand in these new relations to God, angels, and men.[18]

Campbell recognized in the New Testament what has since been called the eschatological dimension—the "even now" and the "not yet." He saw this as applying equally to both the concept of salvation and the kingdom of God.

As the kingdom of Jesus in this world differs from the everlasting

---

[15]MH (1838), 362; for further criticism of this notion of sovereign grace see Ibid (1830), 483; (1831, 27,33; (1833), 493; (1850), 513; (1859), 64, 131

[16]CB (1824), 48

[17]MH (1830), 29-30

[18]Christian System, 161

kingdom of glory, so the salvation of the soul here, and the salvation of the soul and body at the resurrection from the dead, materially differ from each other.[19]

References to the Gospel abound in Mr. Campbell's writings. He gave what may well be his most succinct exposition of the Gospel in the prolegomenon of his "Extra on Regeneration" in 1833. Campbell began by referring to the human condition and to man's need for renewal. Man, despite having inherited a "shattered constitution," is a "proper subject of a remedial system. He is susceptible of renovation." He has been placed under an economy that "contemplates the regeneration of the whole constitution." Jesus is the "model" for this consummated "transformation of spirit, soul, and body." Regeneration thus is eschatological, involving in this life "a renovation . . . of the understanding, will, and affections" and "hereafter. . . a renovation of the body."

While the concern of this essay was tracing the process of regeneration, he wanted at the beginning to set forth the principle underlying the process. What he called "the grand principle, or means. . . for the accomplishment of this moral regeneration is the full demonstration and proof of a single proposition. . . that GOD IS LOVE." To convince men of this truth is the first aim of the Gospel.

At this point Campbell entered into a description of what may be called the psychology of alienation. "Man in a state of alienation and rebellion, naturally suspects, that, if he is a sinner and if God hates sin, he [God] must hate him. . . . and if a sinner suspects that God hates him, he cannot love God." In this state of mind the estranged person "misinterprets every restraint which God has placed in his way to prevent his total ruin, as indicative of the wrath of heaven." As a result there is an increase of alienation and transgression. How then can the goodness of God be known, so as to overcome this state of mind—to produce "repentance and reformation?"

Campbell dismissed the notion that either "the volume of creation. . . or that of God's providence is sufficient to remove . . . these misconceptions, and the consequent alienation of heart." They speak no certain word of the benevolence of God. Only a third volume, the volume of revelation, can supply the means of "learning the true and full character of him against whom we have rebelled"—of revealing "God to man and man to himself." The supreme disclosure of God's love, to which the Bible bears witness, is an event like no other in the history of salvation: the life, death, and resurrection of Jesus Christ.

---

[19]MH (1830), 29. Elsewhere he distinguished between the "present salvation . . . that belongs to the kingdom of grace" and that related to the "new creation. . . the resurrection unto eternal life . . . the kingdom of glory." Ibid., (1831), Extra, 22.

> . . .it is in the person and mission of the INCARNATE WORD that we learn that <u>God</u> <u>is</u> <u>love</u>. That God gave his Son for us, and yet gives his Spirit to us—and thus gives himself—are the mysterious and transcendent proofs of the most august proposition in the universe. The Gospel, heaven's wisdom and power combined, God's own expedient for the renovation of human nature, is no more nor less than the illustration of this regenerating proposition.[20]

Jesus' life and deeds are the "proof, the argument, or the demonstration of that regenerating proposition that presents God and love as two names for one idea."[21]

While the Gospel can be regarded as comprising all the "sayings and doings of Jesus Christ" the decisive facts are those associated with his passion and resurrection; "these group together all the love of God in the gift of his Son;" these were conclusive for Campbell. In an earlier essay he called attention to the fact that Acts, chapter 2, contains no reference to people praying for remission of past sins after the "full revelation of the Gospel of Christ on Pentecost." Rather, said he, "we find them thanking God that he had already, for Christ's sake, forgiven them of all their trespasses."[22]

The foregoing explains the importance he attached to the Gospel as fact—what he later called "<u>kerugma</u>"—in his understanding of the character of revelation. God and his love are known by what he has done.[23] Proclaiming the Gospel facts becomes, therefore, one of the "means of grace."[24]

The above also points to another particular in which Campbell differed from revivalist theory and practice. Revivalists proceeded upon the maxim, long held in the Reformed tradition, that one of the functions of the Law is to convict of sin. Their preaching therefore centered upon the Law, in order to produce what Campbell called a sense of "terror" through which one must pass "before he can believe the gospel." Wrote Campbell: "It is all equivalent to this; that a man must

---

[20]<u>MH</u> (1833), 338-339

[21]<u>Ibid.</u>, (1833), 341

[22]<u>CB</u> (1824), 67

[23]<u>MH</u> (1835), 351

[24]<u>Ibid.</u>, (1833), 341

become a desponding, trembling infidel before he can become a believer."[25] He held the conviction, expressed as early as 1816 in his Sermon on the Law that conviction of sin is produced by the Gospel. The phrase had been misused among most Protestants by being made to apply to actions prohibited by the Decalogue. On the basis of his study of John 16:7-11 Campbell viewed conviction of sin as relating to one's response to the proclamation concerning Jesus. The Spirit would convict the world of sin, righteousness, and judgment "not by applying the law of Moses, but the facts concerning Christ" to the hearer's conscience. He found support for this understanding of John 16:7-11 in the events of the first Pentecost after the resurrection, in the preaching of Prefer and its results.

Appearances to the contrary I believe Campbell was more interested in positive statements of the grace of the Gospel and of the Christian system than in controversy. But the revivals made avoidance of controversy hardly possible. Much of his polemical speaking and writing on our theme related to points at variance between himself and the evangelical mainstream in nineteenth century America, which was basically Reformed in outlook. Still remaining is the task of analyzing his views vis a vis the major trends in the history of the doctrine of justification in the western church. This task is made easier by the recent work of Allister E. McGrath, A History of the Doctrine of Justification (Cambridge, 1986). This author devotes two volumes to a depiction of this development. While we cannot retrace that history here we can draw from his treatment a description of major trends whose light provides perspective for evaluating Campbell's views on the subject.

McGrath's basic contention is that the "articulation of the Christian doctrine of justification" has been dominated by "western concepts of justice," in particular distributive justice, due in large part to a "shift of meaning" that occurred when Hebrew concepts were transferred to a Latin setting.[26] He refers primarily to two Hebrew terms tsedeqah (righteousness) and hatsdiq (to justify).

Tsedeqah has two interrelated meanings: first, being in a right relationship, such as that "presupposed by the covenant between God and Israel" and, second, the behavioral obligations that flow from that relationship. Righteousness and salvation, while not conceptually equated, are "inextricably linked on account of the covenant relationship between God and Israel." However, the meaning of tsedeqah was inadequately expressed when it was rendered by dikaiosune in the Septuagint. Dikaiosune was a "secular concept" which had taken on a meaning "very similar to distributive justice," hence was "incapable of assuming the soteriological overtones" of tsedeqah. The Latin iustitia, used to translate dikaiosune in the

---

[25]CB (1824), 49

[26]McGrath, I, 5

25

Vulgate, had itself acquired a meaning which "encapsulates" the concept of distributive justice—the assessment of rewards or penalties according to merit.[27] Hence it was this concept that governed the thought of the church in the west concerning the meaning of righteousness.

A similar situation obtained for the Hebrew verb hatsdiq (to justify). Its basic meaning is to "'vindicate,' 'to acquit,' or 'to declare to be right.'" However, when hasdiq and the Greek verb dikaioun. used in the Septuagint, were translated into Latin the verb used was instificare, which Latin speaking theologians interpreted as iustum facare ("to do justice").[28]

McGrath views this development as having a debilitating effect upon the church's understanding of justification. Christian thinkers in the west "approached their texts and their subject with a set of propositions which owed more to Latin language and culture than to Christianity itself." There occurred, he writes

> a fundamental alteration in the concepts of 'justification' and 'righteousness' . . . . a shift in emphasis from iustitia coram Deo to iustitia in hominibus . . . .[a] shift in emphasis and reference from God to man. . . accompanied by an anthropocentricity in the discussion of justification which is quite absent from the biblical material. The subsequent development of the theology of justification within the western church would be concerned with the elucidation of this institia in hominibus –i.e., with such questions as: what is the nature of righteousness within man, how did it get there, and where did it come from?[29]

Broadly speaking, the church of Western Europe in the Middle Ages represents one kind of development, the Protestant Reformation represents another. Both, however, worked with the same presuppositions and dealt with the same questions, as above, but came up with different answers.

Medieval theologians, following St. Augustine, regarded justification as a life long process "in which the Christian is made righteous."[30] It involved a fundamental change [ontological] in his nature, hence justification, sanctification,

---

[27]Ibid., I, 8-10

[28]Ibid., I, 14

[29]Ibid., I, 15-16

[30]Ibid., I, 41

and regeneration described the process in its completion.[31] It came about as the result of divine initiative (the infusion of grace) that made possible the human response which in its culmination merits divine acceptance. By the twelfth century a fourfold scheme had become normative, involving the following:

      1. the infusion of grace
      2. the movement of the free will towards God through faith
      3. the movement of the free will directed against sin
      4. the remission of sin[32]

While merit was not considered human achievement apart from grace its retention as associated with justification reflects the hold the concept of "distributive justice" had upon Christian thought.

      Reformation thought continued the view that justification means "to make righteous," but differed from the church of Rome in its understanding of the appropriation of grace to sinners. The following are the "leading primary characteristics of Protestant doctrines of justification. . . over the period 1530-1700" according to McGrath:

      1. Justification is defined as the forensic <u>declaration</u> that the believer is righteous, rather than the process by which he is made righteous. . . .

      2. A deliberate and systematic distinction is made between <u>justification</u> (the external act by which God declares the sinner to be righteous) and <u>sanctification</u> or <u>regeneration</u> as (the internal process of renewal within man. . . .

      3. Justifying righteousness. .. the formal cause of justification is defined as the alien righteousness of Christ, external to man and imputed to him. . . . There is no righteousness within man which can be considered to be the basis of the divine verdict of justification; the righteousness upon which such a judgement is necessarily based is external to man.[33]

Despite controversies within and between the Lutheran and Reformed camps one element is common to Protestantism, the concept of justifying righteousness as being extrinsic—the imputing of the merits of Christ to the believer. In contrast to the medieval view Protestants for the most part insisted upon a distinction between justification (as a forensic declaration) and regeneration (as an inward change).

---

[31]<u>Ibid</u>., I, 48-5

[32]<u>Ibid</u>., I, 44

[33]<u>Ibid</u>., II, 2

Special notice must be taken of developments in the context of Campbell's doctrinal nurture in Northern Ireland, namely the establishment of federal theology as integral to the Westminster Confession of Faith. We noted in our first presentation trends in the Reformed tradition that distanced "Calvinist" theology from Calvin himself—particularly in the dogmatics of Reformed scholasticism. Calvin's Christological emphasis stands in contrast to much Reformed thought in the century and a half that followed. "Personal union" with Christ was for Calvin the key to the understanding of justification. McGrath represents Calvin as follows:

> Justification and sanctification are aspects of the believer's new
> life in Christ, and just as one receives the whole Christ, and not
> part of him, through faith, so any separation of these two
> soteriological elements. . .is inconceivable.[34]

But where Calvin had stressed the role of Christ and the union of the believer with him Reformed dogmatics placed the emphasis upon the divine decrees affecting man's salvation, with a corresponding insistence upon limited atonement.[35]

Federal theology, despite its intention to introduce the element of contingency into the ordo salutis, nevertheless retained the above elements of Reformed theology. A fundamental feature of federal theology was belief that justification rests upon a pretemporal pact between Father and Son in which, in McGrath's words, "God exacted from Christ the condition of perfect obedience to the law in return for the elect as his inheritance."[36] Justification, therefore, consists in the merits of Christ being imputed to the believer, a view which continues the Protestant emphasis upon the alien (extrinsic) righteousness of Christ; but grace is still extended on the basis of the eternal decree of election. Hence federal theology fits McGrath's characterization of Protestantism given above.

This survey, while not exhaustive, nevertheless exposes several crucial issues to which the views of Campbell may be addressed. Fundamental to all these issues and to each approach taken to them is the understanding of the meaning of justification held by its proponents. The same is true for Mr. Campbell. He represents a distinct trend away from the traditional positions characterized by McGrath. The reason for this is that his view of justification more closely resembles the original meaning of tsedeqah than it does the Latinized concept which according to McGrath prevailed in the Middle Ages and still formed the basis for discussion

---

[34]Ibid., II, 37-38; Campbell could have easily adopted this language as his own.

[35]Ibid., II, 40

[36]Ibid., II, 42

in most of Protestantism.

For Campbell justification meant primarily being in right relation to God, a relationship which in every aspect is a matter of grace. Justification and its related themes, he wrote, "represent spiritual relations;" they have to do with the "relation in which my soul stands to God."[37] Incorporation into Christ is decisive in establishing this relationship.[38] This Christological basis was most evident in a statement made to James Wallis of London, England, in 1837:

> The Christian religion is a <u>personal</u> concern. It is confidence in
> a person, love of a person, delight in a person. . . . Jesus Christ
> is the object on which a Christian's faith, hope, and love
> terminate; and to be with Christ is the Christian's heaven.
> Therefore, conversion is a turning to the Lord—in order to which
> Christ must be preached and nothing else.[39]

Justification also relates to man's spiritual condition, his need for restoration—as a correlate of being in right relation to God. In an 1849 discussion of the Trinity (a term he did not like to use, preferring rather to speak of "plurality of existence in the Divine nature"), he declared that the objective of the manifestation of divinity in "these three incomprehensible relationships. . . [was] to effect the complete recovery and perfect redemption of man from the guilt, the pollution, the power, and the punishment of sin."[40]

Moreover, in his view justification carries the implication of behavior appropriate to the believer's relationship to God. The following statement is typical:

> . . .The strongest argument which the Apostles use with the
> Christians to urge them forward in the cultivation and display of
> all the moral and religious excellencies of character are drawn
> from the meaning and value of the <u>state</u> in which they are
> placed.[41]

Relation to God, remission, reform of life, as definitive of justification and its implications for life, find illustration in the following:

> Jesus gives us the philosophy of his scheme in an address to a

---

[37]<u>MH</u> (1831), Extra, 9

[38]<u>Christian System</u>, 161

[39]<u>MH</u>, (1837), 318

[40]<u>Ibid.</u>, (1849), 363

[41]<u>Christian System</u>, 160

sinner of that time—"your sins" says he, "are forgiven you; go and sin no more." He first changes the sinner's state. . . and then says "go and sin no more." He frankly forgave the debt; the sinner loved him.[42]

The understanding of justification as being in right relation to God is reflected in the way he approached the major issues, identified above, that had developed in the history of the doctrine, issues having to do with 1) the use of the metaphor itself; 2) where justification, regeneration, sanctification stand in the ordo salutis; 3) the relation of justification and sanctification; 4) the place, if any, that the concept of merit has as a consideration in the process.

Campbell refused to appeal to a legal frame of references for his understanding of justification. "If a sinner is justified," he declared, "it must be on some other principle than law. He must be justified by favor, and not by right." Still, however, he faced the tension of reconciling the grace of God, exercised in the pardon of sinners, and the righteousness of God—a tension based upon an analysis of Romans 3:25-26, which he called a "profound mystery." How could justification (pardon) be seen as "compatible with the justice, the purity, the truthfulness of God?" This "emergency," as he called it, was met in the unique office of Christ "who by his obedience to that violated law, even unto death" upheld that law and government "so as to open a channel through which truth, righteousness, and mercy can harmoniously flow together and justify God, while justifying the sinner."[43] This he called "evangelical justification" in contradistinction to legal justification.

However, the forensic metaphor applied to justification was unsuitable. It was giving to justification a secular meaning different from the Biblical. In an ancient forum or a modern court justification is a judgment of innocence; whereas "pardons come not to the justified but to the condemned." The Gospel speaks not of acquittal but rather of pardon.[44]

Next, justification, sanctification, regeneration come not as the culmination of a life-long process in which infused grace produces in the cooperative Christian qualities that merit divine acceptance. These terms and others such as reconciliation and adoption describe the "state" or relation of Christians from the very beginning of the life of faith.[45] Campbell noted with a sense of satisfaction that the

---

[42]MH, 1831, Extra, 3

[43]MH (1851), 318-319

[44]Ibid., (1831), 366-376; cf. Christian System, 156

[45]MH (1831), Extra, 9

Westminster Confession of Faith expressed the same view, although he took exception to its identification of sovereign grace with the Holy Spirit's effectual calling of the elect.[46] Nor do the terms justification and sanctification represent forensic judgments, but are rather descriptions of an actual relationship into which one is brought through incorporation into Christ.[47] To be in Christ—to have undergone a "moral and spiritual change" through "the light, the love, the grace of God"[48]—is to be justified, sanctified, reconciled, adopted, saved. These are, he insisted "instantaneous acts of divine grace. . . simultaneous and not successive acts."[49]

> Therefore, said Campbell, it is necessary to distinguish status from character.
> While character is the work of time, a change of state is, or may be, the work of a moment. And while there may be a thousand degrees of comparative excellence in Christian character or of conformity to the perfect model there are no degrees in justification, pardon, or adoption, more than there are in marriage, paternity, fraternity, or citizenship.[50]

These terms represent states or relationships; in character, however, persons in these various states "may be good, better, best, or bad, worse, and worst."[51]

The above may account for the rise of the erroneous notion that Campbell advocated baptismal regeneration. As we have noted above, in his understanding regeneration along with justification and sanctification, represented a state or relationship. Baptism was the culminating act of the process that brought one into that relationship. To those unaware or unappreciative of the distinction he made between state and character and who regarded regeneration as a change of nature wrought by the Holy Spirit it would appear that Campbell was arguing for the efficacy of baptism to bring about what amounted to an ontological change, a notion he would find preposterous. He adamantly insisted upon the necessity of a change

---

[46]Westminster Confession of Faith, Chs XI-XIII; MH (1859), 64

[47]MH (1837), 379

[48]Ibid., (1849), 361

[49]Ibid., (1859), 63

[50]Ibid., (1837), 379

[51]Ibid., (1859), 63

of heart (faith-repentance) as antecedent to baptism.

Sanctification represented a special case for Campbell, however. On the one hand sanctification describes the state of the new Christian.[52] In this respect Campbell differed from much of Protestant thought, which separated the forensic declaration of justification from sanctification (as the internal process of renewal). But at the same time he recognized that in the New Testament sanctification also describes holiness of character.

> To sanctify is to set apart; this may be done in a moment, and so far as mere state, or relation is concerned, it is as instantaneous as baptism. But there is the formation of a holy character: for there is a holy character as well as a holy state. . ... Therefore it is the duty and the work of Christians "to perfect holiness in the fear of the Lord."[53]

Finally, it is obvious from the foregoing that Campbell rejected use of the principle of distributive justice in his understanding of justification. This meant for him that merit, however refined in conception, did not belong to the subject. Persons are accepted into relation to God solely on the basis of grace. They will, as a consequence of their response of faith to divine favor, develop appropriate graces in their lives; but these are the fruit of divine acceptance and not its grounds.

In 1827 a Christian Baptist patron addressed to the editor a query based upon Romans 11:6: "If by grace it is no more of works, otherwise grace is no grace." Campbell's response was short and to the point. "Grace or favor and desert are antipodes. Whatever is of one cannot be of the other. Everything in our salvation is of pure grace."[54]

Mr. Campbell often engaged in controversy over the nature and role of faith and baptism in the morphology of salvation. So much of the rhetoric of revivalist theory centered upon the question: What does God do to save a person? Campbell, assuming the priority of grace, believed the more appropriate question to be that of the Philippian jailer (Acts 16): What must I do to be saved? But as urgent as he felt it was to take up this question and to give it a Biblical answer he never intended that his polemics on this subject would suggest that any merit attached to what one was commanded to do in answer to that question. The following, written in 1859, represents what he had been saying about grace

---

[52] See proposition III of the essay "Remission of Sins," Christian System,
156

[53] Christian System, 49; cf M.H. (1831), Extra, 21

[54] CB (1827), 353

throughout his career.

Grace, like ever other institution, has its own means of development and enjoyment. Hence the means of each and every grace promised and vouchsafed to us are a portion of that Grace itself. The means and the ends are equally the Grace of God. In other words, Faith is a Grace, Repentance is a Grace, Baptism is a Grace, and Regeneration is a Grace. Therefore, our whole salvation is of Grace. There is no human merit in Faith, in Repentance, in Baptism, in Regeneration. They are one and all Divinely bestowed upon man.[55]

---

[55]MH (1859), 132-133

LECTURE III

GRACE AND THE OBEDIENCE OF FAITH

Throughout Christian history practically all churchmen have agreed that both divine grace and human response are involved in man's salvation. Comparatively rare are the two extremes—an emphasis upon grace that makes human response meaningless, on the one hand, or insistence upon the sole efficacy of human action on the other. Nor has there been serious disagreement over what elements enter into man's response to the Gospel, notwithstanding differences among churches in the ordo salutis itself. But there have been differences over what significance to attach to the response of persons to the Gospel. This was a concern which compelled Alexander Campbell's attention, a concern occasioned partly by revival theories of the Second Great Awakening and even more by the Marrow controversy that had erupted in Scotland and Northern Ireland earlier in the century of his birth. The relation of grace and obedience was the chief point at issue in that controversy which, along with the dispute over patronage, was a crucial factor in the forming of the Seceder Church in 1740.

The group known as the Marrow men arose in reaction to the general state of affairs in the Church of Scotland in the early eighteenth century, in what has been described as a somewhat "barren period."[1] Reformed scholastic theology had taken on a harshness that made God an "imperial autocrat"; and federal theology had not proved to be a sufficient corrective. James B. Torrence attributes this state of the church to a type of legalism that had crept into the Scottish Church in the seventeenth century, with the result that the covenant had taken the form of a "contract." He writes:

> The Scottish preacher preached the law in such a way that his concern was to produce a conviction of sin and a fear of judgment, so that he could call upon the sinner to repent and renounce his sin so that he might receive the word of forgiveness and hear the comforts of the Gospel.[2]

---

[1]Stewart Mechie, "The Marrow Controversy Revisited," Evangelical Quarterly (Jan, 1950), 31; cf. W. Beveridge, Makers of the Scottish Church, (Edinburgh, 1908), 175

[2]James B. Torrence, "Covenant or Contract," Scottish Journal of Theology, (Feb. 1970), 58

In other words one's repentance evoked the grace of forgiveness.

Torrence attributes this development in part to a human tendency, exhibited in some sections of early Judaism, but also throughout the history of the church, to turn "God's covenant of grace into a contract," which misses the Biblical idea of grace. While grace is "unconditional in the claims it makes upon us," it is itself "unconditioned—by any consideration of worth in man." In the Biblical idea of covenant, he writes, "the <u>indicatives</u> <u>of grace</u> <u>are</u> <u>always</u> <u>prior</u> <u>to</u> <u>the</u> <u>imperatives</u> of law and human obligation." But this had been reversed to say, in effect, "If you keep the law God will love you," with the result that "the <u>imperatives</u> <u>are</u> <u>made</u> <u>prior</u> <u>to</u> <u>the</u> <u>indicatives</u>. The covenant has been turned into a contract and God's grace made conditional on man's obedience."[3]

Torrence contends that federal theology lies at the root of this tendency to see covenant as contract. The covenant of works given to mankind at creation was a quid pro quo arrangement, linking man's status before God to perfect obedience to the Decalogue. The covenant of redemption made before creation, which issued in the covenant of grace, was itself a conditional agreement between Father and Son that the latter would fulfill the covenant of works on our behalf. As a result it was next to impossible to eliminate from the covenant of grace the implication that God has to be "conditioned into being gracious" and that "forgiveness is made conditional upon repentance."[4]

Many Scottish divines, such as Thomas Boston, had struggled with the question of how to adjust the claims of the Law to a relationship with God based upon grace. The matter was brought to a head in 1717 when the Presbytery of Auchterarder used the following declaration in examination of a candidate for ordination: "It is not sound and orthodox to teach that we must forsake sin in order to come to Christ and to be instated in covenant with God."[5] Upon appeal the General Assembly condemned this proposition as antinomian. Boston, although he felt the Auchterarder article to be poorly worded, believed that it reflected the truth of the Gospel. The Assembly's denunciation of Auchterarder provoked Ralph Erskine to remonstrate: "Some speak of forsaking sin in order to and before coming to Christ. But," said he, "you will never forsake sin evangelically till once Christ come to you and you come to him."[6]

---

[3]Ibid., 56-58

[4]Ibid., 62-63

[5]Mechie, 21; Torrence, 58

[6]Torrence, 58

Boston was responsible for bringing the <u>Marrow of Modern Divinity</u> to bear upon the debate that ensued. He had earlier become aware of the volume and, while impressed with its sentiments, had laid it aside. He now made it available to fellow ministers, and one of them, James Hog, had it printed. It immediately created a storm in the Church of Scotland, with General Assembly arrayed against the Marrow men—a dozen ministers committed to the renewal of the church in terms of insights drawn from the document. A pamphlet war followed. The end result was that in 1720 the volume was condemned as antinomian[7] and ministers forbidden to recommend it. The Marrow men continued their advocacy of the book and this, along with the interest generated by the publicity it received, gave it an even more widespread influence.

The <u>Marrow of Modern Divinity</u> built solidly upon covenant theology in all the essential features of the latter. This is a point of criticism of the Marrow men by Torrence, who states that they did not see that the "legalism against which they were protesting grew in no small measure out of federalism itself."[8] They did, however, reject the distinction between the pre-temporal covenant of redemption and the covenant of grace, so fundamental to the structure of covenant theology, which Torrence sees as the factor which had led to assigning a conditional quality to the latter of the two covenants.[9]

The aim of the <u>Marrow of Modern Divinity</u> was, in the words of Stewart Mechie, "to steer a course between legalism and antinomianism"[10] This was no small task in the light of the conception of the Law set forth in the document. On the one hand the Ten Commandments were the "matter of the covenant of works", still binding upon all mankind although not able to bring life. At the same time the Ten Commandments were the "matter of the law of Christ," serving to define the obligation of the elect to Christ. Although they cannot, as a covenant of works, be a means of attaining life the Ten Commandments still serve as the rule of life for the believer. Thus reads the <u>Marrow</u> in its effort to walk the line that separates legalism and antinomianism:

> The law of Christ in regard to substance and matter is one with
> the covenant of works. . . summed up in the Decalogue. . .

---

[7]John McKerrow, <u>History of the Secession Church</u> (Edinburg, 1847), 12, gives a complete listing of the charges against the Marrow men.

[8]Torrence, 63

[9]<u>Ibid</u>.

[10]Mechie, 20

> commonly called The Moral Law. . . . both these laws agree in
> saying (Doe this) but here is the difference. The one saith (Doe
> this and live) and the other (Live and doe this); the one saith,
> Doe this for life, the other saith, Doe this from life."[11]

One observed the "moral law" out of gratitude. Hence repentance was not for the purpose of disposing God to be gracious but was the response of a grateful heart. Thus the "central theme" of the Marrow was the distinction between legal repentance—fear of hell produced by preaching of the Law—and evangelical repentance, motivated by "gratitude and joy" in response to the message of the cross.[12] These themes of the Marrow of Modern Divinity, as reflected in the Auchterarder "Creed", are what Stewart Mechie describes as the "practical equivalent" of the hymn "Just as I Am."

Campbell's concerns in many respects resemble those of the Marrow men. The Marrow controversy raised issues he had to deal with and undoubtedly served as the backdrop for his own efforts to frame answers to these questions. But neither the Marrow of Modern Divinity nor the controversy to which its name was given defined his stance on the relation of obedience to grace.

On the one hand use of the Decalogue to convict of sin and as the rule of life for Christians had little or no appeal to him. This use of the Law meant that Marrow men, along with federalists generally, tended to think of obedience primarily as obedience to the Law: one could not merit justification by the Law but was still obligated to it as a rule of life. Obedience flowed from gratitude but was defined by the Law. Campbell did not dismiss the Ten Commandments. He found most of them repeated in some form in the New Testament and on that basis still obligatory. But as he insisted in the Sermon on the Law they did not define all Christian obligation. He believed he found the proper basis for defining Christian obligation in the New Testament appeal to adopt a pattern of life in keeping with one's new identity, specifically to take Christ as one's model.

> Feeling himself a son and heir of God, he cultivates the temper,
> spirit, and behavior, which belong to so elevated a relation. . . .
> as the. . . beloved Son of God is to be the model of his future
> personal glory, so the character which Jesus sustained amongst
> men is the model of his daily imitation.[13]

Believers are to be motivated and guided 1) by the "meaning and value of the state

---

[11]Marrow of Modern Divinity, 155-156

[12]Torrence, 59

[13]MH (1833), 356-3357; cf Christian System, 235

in which they are placed,"[14] 2) by the implications of their baptism, and 3) by the nature of their hope.[15]

Again, Campbell distinguished between types of obedience. Like the federalists and the Marrow men who sought to reform them he acknowledged faithful discipleship (the believer's manner of life) as a type of obedience, even though, as above, he appealed to a deeper basis for it. But one's initial response to the Gospel as fact proclaimed (kerugma) was another type of obedience. This represented on his part a different rationale for the understanding of the ordo salutis from that of the tradition in which he had been nurtured. He recognized that most churches included the same elements in their conception of this process. They all emphasized faith, saw a role for the Holy Spirit, repentance, remission of sins, baptism. But there was a great difference in understanding of the order in which each of these elements was seen to stand in the process, which led him to observe that "a different tune is played upon the same notes when the arrangement of them is changed. . . different Gospels are preached from the different ordering of these items."[16] Among mainline Scottish Churches, for example, baptism occurred in infancy. Repentance, precipitated by hearing the Law preached, then faith, came later in life. For Campbell conversion was response to the preaching of Christ (fact—kerugma) not Law, and all these elements—faith, repentance, reformation, and baptism—belong to that response, as a conscious process involving the whole person. This he emphasized as the primary act of obedience and as foundational to all subsequent acts of obedience.

Campbell would have agreed with the Marrow men in rejecting the notion of grace being conditional. Grace is sovereign hence is not evoked by human effort. But he was unwilling to dismiss all discussion of conditions; there were conditions for the enjoyment of grace. Therefore, Campbell sought to clarify the relation between a grace that is unconditional as respects origination yet involving conditions for the appropriation of its benefits. But this in no way implied contract. Contract, as Torrence reminds us, is "a legal relationship in which two parties bind themselves together on mutual conditions to effect some future result."[17] For Campbell recognition of conditions of enjoyment of grace was not a matter of contract. As we noted earlier he made much of the fact that the Biblical record uses

---

[14]Christian System, 60

[15]Ibid., 207

[16]CB (1828), 486-487

[17]Torrence, 54

diatheke, which is unilateral in import, not <u>syntheke</u>, which is bilateral, to refer to covenants initiated by God.

It may be that Campbell's statement of the matter does not differ substantially from Torrence's remark: "The obligations of grace are not conditions of grace."[18] But given the priority of God's love and grace, in what terms should we understand the "obligations" that flow from it? Campbell preferred to speak of "conditions of enjoyment," and sought to discuss the matter in such a way as to safeguard the understanding of grace as unconditioned while stressing human responsibility. In what follows we shall note how he stated the relation between the two.

For Campbell the remedial system, whose goal is to bring man "back to God," involves two elements: What "God has done for us" and what "we must do for ourselves." The initiative lies with God, but human response is necessary to the completion of its objective.

> Heaven. . .overtures, and man accepts, surrenders, and turns to God. Messiah is a <u>gift</u>, sacrifice is a <u>gift</u>, justification is a gift, the Holy spirit is a gift, eternal life is a gift, and even the means of our personal salvation is a gift from God. Truly we are saved by grace. . . . God has provided all these blessings for us, and only requires us to accept of them freely, without any price or idea of merit on our part. But he asks us to receive them cordially, and to give our hearts to him.[19]

In illustration he drew an analogy between the "Kingdom of grace" and the "Kingdom of nature." In the latter God provides the elements that sustain life, "but we must gather and enjoy them." But there is no merit in the gathering or the eating. Likewise no merit attaches to the "eating of the bread of life which came down from heaven for our spiritual life and consolation." But the basic principle remains in both the realms of nature and grace. One must eat the bread provided in order to live. "Hence," he wrote, "there are conditions of enjoyments, though no conditions of merit, either in nature or grace."[20]

Herein lay the significance of Biblical covenants for Campbell. They

---

[18]<u>Ibid.</u>, 56

[19]<u>Christian System</u>, 20-21

[20]<u>Ibid.</u>

embody what God has done or promised (grace) and in most instances[21] what man must do (stipulation). In his view these covenants exhibit a gradual and progressive development of God's plan. They are adapted to the "conditions" of human existence, hence in promise and stipulation show variety as well. However, they share several elements in common: 1) They are all charters of grace or mercy; 2) each has some seal attached, the various seals serving either as monuments of the "facts on which the covenant is founded" or "pledges and seals securing to the covenantees the blessings" of the particular covenant; 3) all required faith and repentance, which, he declared, "are peculiar to no dispensation of religion." Hence, obligation is a feature of each covenant, although not itself evoking the grace upon which covenantal promise is based. Wrote Campbell

> There is no covenant of redemption based upon human effort or human merit. All God's overtures are the offspring of pure unmerited favor. The conditions propounded are not merely to justify God before the universe. . . but benevolence requires that man should believe what God says, feel in harmony with all his requisitions, and obey from his heart every precept.[22]

Not unrelated to covenant as illustrative of what God has done and what man must do is Campbell's classification of the blessings of the King of Heaven as antecedent and consequent, which he identified as follows:

> The antecedent includes all those blessings bestowed on man to prepare him for action and to induce him to action. The consequent are those which God bestows on man through a course of action correspondent to those antecedent blessings.

Adam, Abraham, and Israel are cases in point. In each instance an act or acts of God came prior to any response expected of the beneficiary. He found God's dealings with Abraham and Israel to be particularly informative, in that elective grace preceded and made possible their response of faith.

> All that God did for Abraham in promise and precepts before his obedience—and all that he did for the Israelites in bringing them up out of Egypt and redeeming them from the tyranny of Pharaoh—was antecedent to the duties and observances which he enjoined upon them.

The antecedent blessings became the occasion and supplied the motive for their

---

[21]Exceptions are the covenant with Noah, the promise to Abraham, and the covenant with David, which contained no stipulations.

[22]MH (1846), 263-264

response of faith and determined the form that response should take.[23]

Likewise, in the Kingdom of Heaven (the new covenant) there are both antecedent and consequent blessings. The "antecedent blessings are the constitution [covenant] of grace, the King and all that he did, suffered, and sustained for our redemption. . . . This is all favor, pure favor, sovereign favor. . . . But the remission of sins, our adoption into the family of God. . . are consequent upon faith and the obedience of faith."[24]

Moreover, fact (the acts of God in Christ), promise, and stipulation made up the substance of the preaching of the Apostles and early evangelists. Campbell's summary of Peter's sermon on the first Pentecost after the resurrection resembles C. H. Dodd's outline of the kerygma. The following is taken from the Campbell-Rice debate. Peter's address on Pentecost, said he, is

> a synopsis of the whole evangelical economy. It is based on three facts which transpired on earth—the death, burial, and resurrection of the Messiah; and on three facts which transpired afterwards—his ascension, coronation, and reception of the Holy Spirit, for the consummation of the objects of his reign. The precepts are also three—believe, repent, and be baptized. The promises are three—remission of sins, the Holy Spirit, and eternal life.[25]

Campbell only had to import one item in order to keep intact the series of three's he used in exposition of Peter's sermon. He based his understanding of the relation of human action to the divine initiative upon analysis of this and other occasions of proclaiming the Gospel in the book of Acts. In each instance commands in keeping with the content of the Gospel and appropriate to the conditions of the hearers were part of the proclamation itself. The Gospel, he wrote, "has in it a command and as such must be obeyed;" thus he identified "obedience of the Gospel" and "the obedience of faith."[26]

Campbell analyzed Acts 2 in still another way—on the basis of "common sense" psychology. He used the same terms to describe the process on Pentecost as would apply whenever persons become aware of some fact of existence that carries

---

[23]Christian System, 149-150

[24]Ibid., 150. Campbell would resist any suggestion that this is a contractual arrangement.

[25]Debate between Rev. A. Campbell and Rev. N. L. Rice, 435.

[26]Christian System, 165-166

great meaning to them. In such a case the fact elicits a response in keeping with the meaning it has for those persons and thus exhibits what Campbell would call a "cause and effect" relationship; that is, action producing "corresponding action." His summary, which applied to facts not open to immediate observation, describes the process in five words: fact, testimony, faith, feeling, action, which he explained as follows:

> Fact . . . is anything said or done; testimony is the representation
> of it in words; faith, the belief of these words; feeling, the force
> and power of these words; and action, the effect of them.[27]

He saw this order clearly at work on Pentecost: Peter's witness to the life, death, and resurrection of Christ evoked faith and intense feeling in his hearers, who were then called upon to act: "Reform and be baptized." He made frequent use of this schema for describing the working of the good news in human experience. Going a step further, he saw this arrangement as the love of God made operative in human redemption. These five terms, he wrote

> represent the same thing [God's love] in five attitudes. . . . the
> gift of Jesus is the love of God in fact, the report of it is the love
> of God in word or testimony; the belief of it is the love of God in
> our faith; the feeling of repentance, gratitude and is the love of
> God in feeling; and our obedience to all divine precepts and
> promises is the love of God in action.[28]

Elsewhere he stated that when our response to the Gospel is understood in these terms obedience is "natural."[29]

The Gospel, then, calls for a response of the whole person. In commenting on Romans 10:9-10: "With the heart man believeth unto righteousness, and with the mouth confession is made unto salvation" Campbell noted that what this passage calls for is commitment of the whole person to Christ.

> I value not, and will never plead for, anything under the name of
> religion, which does not influence the head, the heart, the tongue,
> the lips, the hands, the feet—the whole body, soul, and spirit.[30]

He was disturbed by the disparagement of baptism by many churchmen of his day. Particularly offensive was the reference to baptism as a "mere bodily act,"

---

[27]MH (1837), 531

[28]Ibid.

[29]Ibid., (1833), 350

[30]Ibid., (1830), 28

which seemed to set in contrast overt action and faith, as though they could be separated in human behavior. This expression was used by Andrew Broaddus in a critique of Campbell's "Extra on Remission of Sins."[31] Campbell responded to Broaddus in an article, "Extra Defended,"[32] but dealt more extensively with this issue four years later in the <u>Christian System</u>. Here he insisted that baptism

> into the name of the Father, the Son, and the Holy spirit is an act
> of the whole man—body, soul, and spirit. The soul of the
> intelligent subject is as fully immersed <u>into</u> the <u>Lord Jesus</u>, as his
> body is immersed <u>in the water</u>. His soul rises with the Lord Jesus,
> as his body rises out of the water.[33]

He went on to warn: "Reader, be admonished how you speak of bodily acts in obedience." He cited a number of Old Testament personages whose notoriety rested upon their deeds, alluding finally to the "sacrifice of a body on Mount Calvary." He concluded by saying: "There is no such thing as outward bodily acts in the Christian institutions; and less than in all others, in the act of immersion."[34]

Campbell found a still more comprehensive example of the way of salvation in the Biblical teaching concerning justification—an example he repeated several times in his writings. His examination of scripture pointed to a number of "causes" to which to ascribe justification: faith, grace, the blood of Christ, works, the name of the Lord Jesus, and knowledge, each prefaced by the phrase "justified by. . . ." He cited Isaiah 53:11 for reference to justification by knowledge on the ground that this passage was Messianic in import. He saw all these elements as interrelated:

> We have the grace of God as the <u>moving</u> cause, Jesus Christ for
> the <u>efficient</u> cause, his blood the <u>procuring</u> cause, the name of the
> Lord the <u>immediate</u> cause, faith the <u>formal</u> cause, and works for
> the <u>concurring</u> cause.

He constructed a parable to illustrate the interrelation of these elements:

> A gentleman on the seashore describes the wreck of a vessel at
> some distance from the land. . . and covered with a miserable and
> perishing sea-drenched crew. Moved by pure philanthropy, he
> sends his son in a boat to save them. When the boat arrives at the

---

[31]<u>Ibid.</u>, (1830)

[32]<u>Ibid.</u>, (1831)

[33]<u>Christian System</u>, 215

[34]<u>Ibid.</u>, 216

> wreck, he invites them in upon the condition that they submit to
> his guidance. A number of the crew stretch out their arms, and
> seizing the boat with their hands, spring into it, take hold of the
> oars, and row to land. . . . The <u>moving</u> cause. . . was the good
> will of the gentlemen on the shore; the son. . . was the <u>efficient</u>
> cause; the boat itself the <u>procuring</u> cause; the knowledge of their
> perishing condition and his invitation, the <u>disposing</u> cause; the
> seizing of the boat. . . and springing into it, the <u>immediate</u> cause;
> their consenting to his condition, the <u>formal</u> cause, and the
> rowing to shore under the guidance of the Son, the <u>concurring</u>
> cause of their salvation.

All these elements were involved, as are all those to which justification is attributed.
Hence, he declared, it is a mistake to affix the term <u>alone</u> to any one of the
seven—as many of his contemporaries were doing in the case of faith. Faith is only
one of three instrumental "causes"; why, he asked, emphasize faith as the justifying
factor to the exclusion of, or in preference to, the others?[35]

Although he rejected the concept of "faith alone," Campbell still
recognized the primacy of faith in motivating and guiding the response of persons
to God's initiative in redemption. In his essay, "Remission of Sins, " in contrasting
the obedience of faith and the obedience of law, he wrote" "faith in God's promises
through Jesus Christ. . . [is] the principle from which obedience flows."[36] In another
instance, in exposition of the nature of faith in Romans 4, he affirmed an
indissoluble relation between faith and obedience. On the one hand faith is
"indispensable to the enjoyment of every blessing connected to the ordinances of
the Gospel. At the same time it is only through obedience to what he called "these
gracious institutions" that faith is perfected.[37]

There is still another element that motivates obedience which is both prior
to faith and its basis, namely, what he called the antecedent blessings of the
Kingdom—acts of God expressive of his grace. "<u>God never commanded a being to
do anything</u>," he wrote, "<u>but the power and motive were derived from something
God had done for him</u>." By this he meant the "free and sovereign favor" of God. It
is faith, motivating obedience to this grace, that brings one to the enjoyment of the

---

[35]<u>Ibid</u>., 216-217; Campbell was fond of this allegory. He first used it in
<u>MH</u> (1831) Extra, 41-41, and again in <u>MH</u> (1851), 321

[36]<u>Christian System</u>, 166

[37]<u>MH</u> (1857), 648

so-called consequent blessings of life in the Kingdom.[38]

The examples given above show that Campbell regarded obedience as necessary. At the same time he saw no merit in anything man was called upon to do in response to God's invitation in the Gospel. He was quite explicit in this matter. "Our whole salvation is of grace," said he. "there is no human merit in Faith, in Repentance, in Baptism, in Regeneration. They are one and all divinely bestowed upon man." He likened this matter to such physiological functions as breathing, eating, sleeping. These processes do not by their exercise create the element whose assimilation is essential to the health of the body.[39]

Campbell is known for his efforts to clarify and defend his understanding of the New Testament institution of baptism. It was the subject of three of his major debates, reflecting the importance the subject had for him in considering the basic order of the church. Of equal importance was proper understanding of baptism in the ordo salutis. However, his debates and discourses on this subject were not aimed directly at making converts but to clarify the process for those so engaged. For example, in the conclusion of his essay on "Regeneration" he asserted that no one is converted by a theory of regeneration. It is "preposterous" to preach the theory of regeneration in order to convert the hearers. The treatise containing the theory was written "for the benefit of those who are employed in the work of regenerating others" and to correct the notion held by some that he regarded baptism as the only requisite to "the whole process of conversion or regeneration."[40]

In his debates with W. L. McCalla (1823) and N. L. Rice (1843) he affirmed the proposition that baptism is for the remission of sins. It was one of the ordinances given to "consummate" or to "perfect" justifying faith. But, he continued, the merit is not in these ordinances. They are means of "enjoyment" or reception of grace. While grace and works are "incompatible. . . grace and baptism into Christ are not. . . for baptism is not a work of the subject but of the administrator. . . . These can be no merit in a work not performed by the subject himself." The same applies to deeds performed in behalf of fellow men. They are "radiations of philanthropy," expressive of gratitude to God, and not means of incurring his favor. "We can never make God our debtor."[41]

I made reference in my second lecture to an 1827 statement of Campbell:

---

[38]Christian System, 150

[39]MH (1859), 133

[40]Christian System, 238

[41]MH (1857), 648-649

"Grace or favor, and desert are antipodes." He appended to this statement a parable built around the gift of property by a person identified as "A" to one identified as "B." He might well have reversed the figures to have "B" as the donor—"B" representing his father-in-law John Brown, who made such a gift to Alexander and Margaret early in their marriage. Although brief it sets forth Campbell's view of grace and works:

> A. by a mere act of favor, or deed of gift, invests B. with a large farm amply sufficient for the purposes of life. He afterwards writes him a letter, informing him that if he does not take exercise, if he does not mingle labor and rest, and avoid every excess, he cannot live or be happy. Now he that argues that B. obtained the estate by his works is in error; and everyone who says that, without the works enjoined by A. in his epistle, B. can live and be happy is in error; and everyone who says that B. got the farm as a reward of his works says what is not true.[42]

Campbell's understanding of the relation of divine grace and human obligation can be summarized in two statements, which apply either to one's initial response to the Gospel or to one's manner of life as a child of God.[43] First, there are no conditions for the "procurement" of grace, that is, to evoke the grace of God. Neither in the kingdom of nature or the kingdom of grace does "he act of being born" purchase or procure life. Secondly, there are conditions for the enjoyment of grace. "All the means of salvation are means of enjoyment not of procurement." Still they are necessary; "if the child is never born," he wrote, "all its sensitive powers and faculties cannot be enjoyed."[44] Campbell was willing to acknowledge the validity of "Just as I Am," with the qualification of faith in the person and mission of Jesus and willingness to submit to his Lordship.[45]

Grace is sovereign, hence unconditioned, but it is not without obligations. There are conditions for enjoyment of its benefits, conditions defined by the nature of grace itself as exhibited in the Gospel, and therefore aspects of the grace itself.[46]

---

[42]CB (July, 1827), 353

[43]For examples of the latter see Christian System, 20-21, 148, 233.

[44]Ibid., 20-21

[45]Ibid., 212

[46]MH (1859, 131-133; here Campbell stated that the "means of each and every grace promised and vouchsafed to man are a portion of that grace itself."

Obedience, however, is not to be seen as making ourselves acceptable (which is legalism) or as disposing God to be gracious or accepting.

The distinction between the "obligation of grace" and the "conditions of grace," while real, is not easily drawn. The atmosphere of nineteenth century America, which included such things as the revivals and the hold that federal theology had upon Reformed thought, made communication of his views difficult for Campbell. Revivalists for the most part identified grace as the direct operation of the Holy Spirit upon depraved man, hence placed major emphasis upon what God does to save sinners. In Campbell's view God had already done something, the Gospel being witness. The question now was: what must I do? He addressed himself to answering that question, a not too welcome approach in that context.

Moreover, Campbell viewed regeneration primarily as indicative of the new state of one in Christ. Most revivalists saw it as signifying an ontological change preparatory to faith. Hence Campbell's view of baptism as the culmination of the process of the new birth was interpreted as ascribing efficacy to the water of baptism, resulting in the charge that he taught "water regeneration," a notion that was repugnant to him.

His debates were complicating factors in that they focused upon specific points at issue in understanding Gospel commands more than upon the entire scheme of redemption in which grace plays the major role. Hence the debates afforded little opportunity for setting forth his total view of the relation of grace and obedience.

In addition very few in the Reformed tradition were willing to consider the distinction of covenants he made in the Sermon on the Law.[47]

Campbell's views on this subject did not change substantially over the years; but in his writings in the 1850's one senses a concern on his part to express more emphatically his conviction that, notwithstanding the necessity of obedience, the priority remains with grace—as it must if by the term grace we are describing God. He would have been appalled by the trend later in the Stone-Campbell movement to view covenant as a quid pro quo arrangement—to regard obedience as a means of achieving acceptability. A. T. De Groot had this development in mind when he credited Isaac Errett, one of Campbell's immediate successors, for saving

---

[47]Hillyer H. Straton, pastor of Trinity Baptist Church, Malden, Mass., in a 1969 article "Alexander Campbell's Influence on the Baptists," (Encounter (Fall, 1969), 365, speaking of the Sermon on the Law asserted: "Here is expounded in one of the best statements written the anti-legalism which is at the very heart of Baptist philosophy and raison d'etre. Alexander Campbell . . . was entirely too brilliant a man to hold to the legalism of a water salvation. Baptists must believe him when he says this . . . ."

the movement of his day "from becoming a fissiparous sect of jangling legalists."[48] A litany of examples could be cited, which is a chapter in itself. I call attention to a few.

1. The tendency to present the goals of the Movement in terms either of restoration only or unity only, which in effect places the claims of truth above the claims of grace, or vice versa. "Grace and truth came by Jesus Christ;" so states John's Gospel. Unfortunately the disciples of Jesus often seem unable to hold the two together in conducting the affairs of the Kingdom.

2. Another concern is raised by James B. Torrence regarding worship in the Church of Scotland in the post-Westminster era. Treating covenant as contract resulted in what he calls an "impoverishment of worship" in that emphasis was placed more upon what man does in worship than upon the "continuing high priesthood of Christ." We of the Stone-Campbell Movement may do well to ask whether our type of emphasis upon the prophetic office of Jesus (in the preaching) and upon his Lordship—both of which are proper and necessary—has been matched by a corresponding emphasis upon his present office of making intercession for us.

3. A tendency in preaching to focus more upon the "imperative of obedience" than upon the "indicatives of grace." I borrow this phrasing from Torrence who sees it as descriptive of the church in the eighteenth and nineteenth centuries and extending to the present. He brands it as an inversion of the evangelical order that occurs when covenant is treated as contract.[49] Surely emphasis on obedience is proper in Christian communication; but separated from the affirmations of the grace of the Gospel it may encourage the notion that obedience is a way of gaining merit.

4. Equally serious is the current tendency to see grace as involving no imperatives at all. Once in a class lecture I made reference to Jesus' statement: "Except a grain of wheat fall into the earth and die. . . ." I pointed out that Jesus applied this metaphor not only to himself but to his followers. One of the students of the class, who was caught up in the frenzy of the "Jesus Movement" of the early 1970's retorted: "If I talked that way to people I could never win them to Christ!"

5. Alongside the above is the tendency that establishes an almost mechanical relation between obedience and the enjoyment of the benefits of God's favor. In one instance the baptism of a newly professed convert was delayed until the evening service. A deacon indignantly demanded to know: "What if she were to die before the evening service?" He sincerely believed that in such a case she

---

[48]W. E. Garrison and A. T. De Groot, <u>Disciples of Christ, A History</u> (1948) 358

[49]Torrence, 66-70

would not be saved.

6. Perhaps most disturbing is the notion that by our obedience we are achieving acceptability or disposing God into being accepting. I recall a tract written some years ago setting forth what its author called the "Plan of Salvation." In his statement concerning baptism he declared, "Now God changes his mind toward the sinner."

7. Almost tragic is the uncertainty this attitude fosters in the hearts of believers as to whether they have been truly forgiven. The following is an extreme case but illustrates the point. An aged saint who had served the church sixty-five of her eighty years, while lying on the bed of her final illness, cried out in anguish: "Have I done enough?"

This recital could go on. One could hope that these instances were exceptional. I fear they are not.

The attitude I am describing may be due to the almost universal tendency to regard precepts and norms not so much as expressive of the love and concern of their author and as appropriate responses to his love, but rather as conditions for being loved. It may also be attributed to failure to draw clearly the line between a grace for which there are no conditions of procurement and the conditions for the enjoyment of that grace.

In conclusion, it might be well to suggest, as the second best of several options, a re-reading of Campbell on this subject; the first option, of course, being a re-reading of the New Testament itself in its witness to the grace of God.